I AM THE SUN

SHREEYA DESAI

Illustrations by:
Pinterest Creators

A book must be an axe for the frozen sea within us
- Franz Kafka

I AM THE SUN

Darling your existence is proof that Perfect exists
Your heart is full of fire
You don't know why you constantly burn
You are the fuel itself
A force that desires to ignite a flame so big,
it would burn everything to ashes
You are war itself
The one who fights endlessly for others
You don't tire
You're a craving of all the impulses
Others cannot understand you because
You were born indestructible

Shreeya Desai

I'm sorry you have to work through the aftermath
of the pain planted by someone else
I'm sorry you have to sew up the wounds you didn't create
You are a nice person in an awful world
This world has nothing good except you
It's only war, bloodshed, manipulation, cheating and hate
The tiger stripes across your body is a sign of strength
I see the wild in your eyes
And the passion in your belly
You are the earthquake
Bringing mountains to their knees

I AM THE SUN

People want to hear poetry with the words
they hesitate to say
We all are like little dandelions drifting in the wind
Scattering seeds of love into the unknown
Hoping one of them would find a place to grow
and call home

Shreeya Desai

Most people think hope is fragile and timid
She's not
Even if all the world tries to push her down
She will not silence her voice
Those lips are not here just to be pretty
Change looks like her
She will stand against the
dread-bolted thunder
and rise from the ashes
With her blood stained knuckles
She fights again and again
You will fear the cold
and crave the burn

I AM THE SUN

There Is a flower that blooms amidst darkness and despair
That flower is a spark of hope
That even in the darkest times
We too have the ability to bloom
So when we feel the weight of the night
And the darkness clouds our thoughts
Remember the flower that blooms in the night
Each of its petal burning bright

Shreeya Desai

And when I take a peek into your soul
I see the colors
that bleed out of your heart
The light that won't be dimmed
Like the sirens of the sea
The tracks of your unshed tears
On your saccharine skin
I will make sure to hold you
amidst the chaos
For you are the language of the flowers
And getting away from you is like
Washing away the salt from the sea

I AM THE SUN

The night is covered in blood
And tragedies of your estrangement
Knaw at your soul
When It all feels like an endless stretch of blue
I want you to know that
Nobody is half as bright as you
The ocean of emotions you swallow
As you carry your burdens
I promise to be the one to dry your eyes
When you fall apart

Shreeya Desai

I have licked the stains off the knife that stabbed me
And danced in the ashes
Of the broken glass pieces of my heart
The blood of my soul forming a shield
You cannot hurt me
I was born of the sea
With claws and teeth
And impatient legs
I am my own devastating deity

I AM THE SUN

You shouldn't have to endure someone's torment to know that they love you

I think we have got the definition of nice very wrong. Being nice doesn't mean you're gonna let people walk over you like a doormat. That is called being stupid. Being nice means taking a stand for yourself.

Your bones won't crumble if you do.
Bare your teeth and go for the throat.

I AM THE SUN

If only we saw each others souls
In stead of our bodies
The world would be a different place altogether
Switch on the wipers and clear the minds mirror
Why does this obstinate voice in our head torment us so much?

Shreeya Desai

This body is my home
My childhood is buried here
Every memory, every thought and every person I've crossed paths with
Rests here
Clotting in my veins
Numbing my soul
Do not try to hurt me
For this body of mine is sacred
I will take a crowbar and pry it in your gut
And carve my way out
I will walk to the ends of the world just to save myself

I AM THE SUN

The world has taught you only to be rough
never will you be gentle again
Knuckles always bloody and elbows bruised
You are reckless and distant
My Golden Child
Who made you think you deserve all that?
Who will you pray to now?
How many times will you repent?
Are you still fighting for your peace?

Tell me how do I dilute someone ?

Shreeya Desai

I am the force of nature
The eye of the hurricane
In the ashes of destruction,
You'll find my name
I will turn my scars into stars
And wield a sword into my fate
I am the wrath of the storm
I don't need to recuperate

I AM THE SUN

Do not afraid to be bitter
May thunder be your voice
Heart beating like a drum
You are a beacon of strength
The face of rage
A hedonistic goddess
Let them choke on the words they said to you
You are the devil they forgot
born with pearl teeth
And stripes across your face
You can only extinguish the fire if you starve it of oxygen

The mess you have made is nothing but magical
Shout obscenely
Spill what's in your guts
Hunt the flame
In the end we all just turn into stories in someone's book

I AM THE SUN

You do no have to walk on your knees
Tell me about your despair and ill tell you mine
There is violence in reconstruction
You dont have to give shape to this sorrow, rage, and loss
A little far off the beaten path
The sun keeps rising and bushes keep bearing the fruit
As erudite as you may be
You think youre only a dictionary of obsecure sorrows
Maybe its because you forget that
To be the sun you have to burn first

Shreeya Desai

On days that you find yourself tossing and turning in bed
Remember you divinity
Woven in your veins
It walks with your shadows
Feel it engulf you
It is time for you to grow your wings
You are nothing but a flame
Ever so flickering
Stay as you are
The master of your destiny
You have suffered enough, you deserve a good epilogue

I AM THE SUN

They say the man in me is lost
I say
Watch me save him
Oh sweetheart, even Rome fell
And my spirit of light
no one can take that away
I know that hell must break loose
For it to pass
So I will scream till all my demons have been silenced
I will work
As my spine breaks
I am untamable
This is the alchemy of my hands

Perhaps my skin will forgive me for the scars I made
I am sorry I didn't love you like I loved the other parts of me
But every night I promise myself
That I am loved beyond measure
And I will take good care of my heart
I will rise on my own
I'm the sun, I heal, I burn

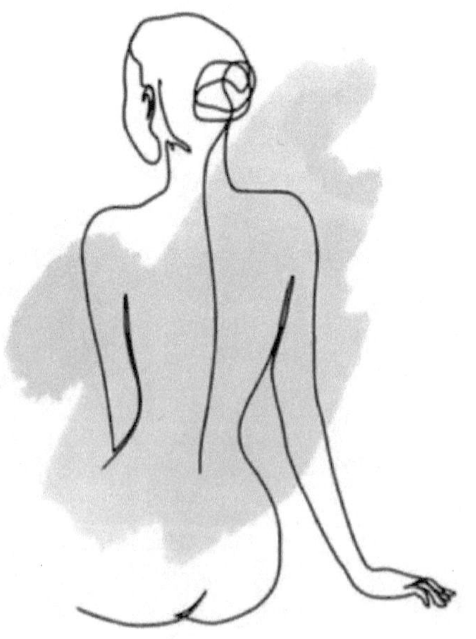

I AM THE SUN

Everywhere we look
There's shooting stars and fireflies
The complex magic of nature constantly blazes before our eyes
And yet you believe fairytales don't exist?

Shreeya Desai

I will not unzip my chest to every person I meet
I will not dress me up in a bow and present myself to you
I will not wear a blanket of acceptance

In the grey mist of my own thoughts
I remember what my bones have been through

I will take my mind off it's iron cage
And let my spirit roar

now I grow wings

Shreeya Desai

Oh tell me atlas, how do you bear the weight of the world?
How is it you stand through the stormy nights
And still find a way to heal

Do you draw strength from the sea?
Or from dreams of humanity?

Oh tell me atlas, how do you bear the fire of a thousand hearts?
As our tears fall like rain
How do you hold the heavens and the earth?

When I was done trying to die
With a heart that beats though bruised and sore
I found you atlas

The guardian of the world
The canvas of seas
You hold pages filled with cities
You bring us hope

I AM THE SUN

What they cannot understand is how you didnt break, leak or splatter yet
Just a drop of blood is all theyre waiting to point fingers at
A sonic boom
A new way to burn down your house
But darling,
They dont know what you are capable of
The only savior I believe in is me

You are brilliant even in your decent to madness

www.ingramcontent.com/pod-product-compliance
Lightning Source LLC
LaVergne TN
LVHW091244150826
845673LV00003B/1292